PALMISTRY

How to know yourself, develop potentialities, assess love, marriage and career prospects, by interpreting 'the map you'll never lose' – hand markings, fingers and thumbs – in accordance with the ancient laws of palmistry.

By the same author:

NUMEROLOGY: The Secret Power of
  Numbers
COLOUR HEALING: Chromotherapy and
  How it Works

PALMISTRY

Your Destiny in Your Hands

by

MARY ANDERSON

THE AQUARIAN PRESS
Wellingborough, Northamptonshire

First published 1973
This Edition 1980
Second Impression 1982
Third Impression 1984
Fourth Impression 1985

ISBN 0 85030 164 5 (UK)
ISBN 0 87728 406 7 (USA)

Printed and bound in Great Britain by
Richard Clay (The Chaucer Press) Limited,
Bungay, Suffolk.

CONTENTS

CHAPTER ONE

THE MAP YOU'LL NEVER LOSE

Palmistry has always had an unfailing amusement value. The hand reader is in demand at Christmas parties, to say nothing of the summer resort palmists, some of whom within the limits of their own background, are surprisingly good. It is precisely this entertainment side of palmistry which tends to bring it into disrepute in scientific circles.

However, as with all the occult sciences there has always been an esoteric or inner and an exoteric or outer body of knowledge; the latter fulfilling a definite human need to know the future and have answered such questions as: will I get married? be rich? famous? have children and be happy?

Rooted in Antiquity

But palmistry in terms of value goes deeper than this, its roots lie buried deep in antiquity. The ancient courts of kings had their wise men or soothsayers and they advised and warned from their knowledge of the stars and the signs and symbols which they read in the hands of men. In many countries, spiritual leaders were recognized by the signs on their hands.

According to the ancient teachings of occultism, man represents the microcosm – the small world, or the universe – the macrocosm. Everyone carries the map of their life in the palm of their hand, read aright it can unlock the mystery of destiny.

However, to the present position, Dr Charlotte Wolff who has studied hands from the point of view of psychological diagnosis answers most clearly the sceptic's query: why should there be anything in it? and she writes: 'The hand is a visible part of the brain'.

This then is the reply to those who are puzzled as to why the shape, crease-lines and markings of the hand should provide information as to the character, personality and abilities of a person.

So the real value of palmistry is to help us to know ourselves and in this way to develop our potentialities, recognize our limitations and so enable us to make the best use of what we have, directing our talents into ways of all round fulfilment and happiness.

Control of Destiny

It can also help us in our human relations, to understand our relatives and friends, we gain insight through understanding and we may even be able to control our destiny by applying the knowledge gained with foresight to the understanding of all our human problems.

At the time of writing the medical world is taking an increasing interest in the study of hands and disease so that it is now possible to ascertain certain inherent weaknesses through the study of the hands of a new-born baby.

Dr C.G. Jung gave his approval to palmistry and wrote, '... the findings and knowledge are of essential importance for psychologists, doctors and educationists. It is a valuable contribution to a character research in its widest application.'

On a more everyday level this little book may help you to evaluate.:

Your own individuality, find yourself.
Your emotional nature – love, affection, sexual response, marriage.
Your success potential.
Your talents, creativity – imagination.
Your success in business and other enterprises.
Likelihood of fame, recognition.
Other indications to fulfilment, life experience, travel possibilities, spiritual development.

Destiny versus Free Will

In a book which deals with an assessment of personality through esoteric knowledge we always come up against the question of Destiny versus free will.

It is the author's contention that certain factors are predestined, after all so far as you know you did not ask to be born. In palmistry, the left hand is always considered to be the hand of the inherited constitution and characteristics, so the destiny we are born with; but the right hand shows the way in which our inheritance is used. Those who are naturally left-handed must reverse this dictum.

So that while we live and have our being within the pattern of our destiny, our reactions to the blows or favours of fate are within our own control and it is to this extent that we control our destiny. It is only too true to say that our lives, and environment, material, physical and emotional are but projections of our own natures.

Where we feel that we have been unfortunate we have to think about the necessity of change within ourselves, a willingness to change our attitudes, to be positive and courageous and experience life to the full. Only a change within ourselves will change what we are pleased to call 'our luck' for the better.

A fair understanding of palmistry can first of all give us insight into ourselves and others, secondly it can provide a great deal of interest and entertainment, thirdly, carefully studied over a period of years it can help in vocational guidance. It can be a guide to the choice of marriage partner, an aid in seeing how to handle and direct children, later can assist in planning their career and in medical circles can be used to indicate the early stages of certain illnesses.

In everyday life it can be helpful in understanding strangers, for as you study hands and gesture you will begin to get an insight into the person you are dealing with, whether this is an acquaintance, an employer or an employee.

Finally, it can become a lifetime study of great value and help you to develop not only insight, but also your E.S.P. faculties and sensitivity.

CHAPTER TWO

FIRST STEPS

In order to be good at hand reading you have first of all to have a liking for people, then you must cultivate your powers of observation. You observe people, how they sit, how they stand and how they hold their hands.

Your first contact may be the handshake and this will tell you quite a lot about the person and the information you gain can be included in your reading.

The handshake can be firm, indicating a firm positive, outgoing character, moist and clinging, an indeterminate, maybe weak type, a quick sharp squeeze, someone who is often in a hurry and cannot bother to pay attention to the little things in life.

You watch and you see how people hold their hands, if the hands give a relaxed easy impression, either placed on the chair arms or in the lap.

Do they fidget with their fingers or with anything available? These are nervous tensed up people.

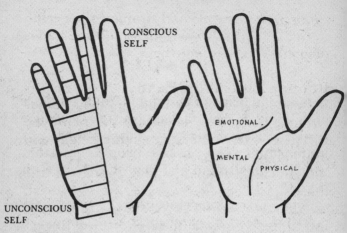

Do they wave their hands about when they talk, illustrating everything with their hands? They are the voluble, talkative people who often 'tell all'.

Do they hide their hands or one hand in their pocket. These are people who are secretive or self-conscious.

While most people are only too anxious for you to read their hands, you will encounter the odd type who will firmly refuse and stuff their hands into their pockets, resisting the beguiling attempts of their friends to 'have a go'. These are the people who have deep seated fears and one of these is that they might get to know themselves.

However, in general you will find that people thrust their hands at you palm up. It

is wise, in order to avoid strain to the person
to find a table or something to rest the hands
on while you examime them.

Routine for Reading Hands

1. Ask the person to hold up their hands
with the back towards you. At this point you
can assess the size relative to the height and
build of the person.

You can also assess the spread of the
fingers, are they held together, spread apart,
do they curl inwards to the palm? Is the
index finger longer than the third finger?
What about the thumb, is it long, broad, how
is it held, close to the hand or wide apart?
2. Feel the hand for breadth, width, colour,
shape, length of fingers, are these flexible or
stiff? Are the fingers knuckled? What basic
shape is the hand and what are the finger tip
and nail shapes? Are there any peculiarities
as to the nails or the straightness or
otherwise of the fingers?
3. Turn the hands over and examine the
lines starting with the Life line, the Head line
and the Heart line, in that order.

Then examine the line of Fate, the line of
Sun and the line of Health.
4. Look at the Mounts and their
development and associate them with the
relevant fingers.

5. Look at the Mount of Venus, the Girdle of Venus and the Lines of Affection to tell the tale of the affections, co-ordinating it with your assessment of the Heart line and the general hand appearance.

6. Look for lucky signs on the hands, make your reading positive and encouraging. Look for the money signs, the lucky 'M' and the Triangle and the Angle of Luck.

Finally, if you think that you see an adverse happening on the hand, never state baldly, 'It looks as if you'll have a serious accident about 45', etc.

The value of palmistry lies in warning and encouraging. More harm has been done by such Jonahs than can be truly assessed, often the professional palmist sees the sad results years later.

Never Predict Death

If you see what you think is an adverse mark, whether it refers to accident or illness, put it tactfully and helpfully and *never* predict death. If you see what you think is an accident mark and the hand is generally of an impulsive type, you can warn by saying, 'I think you are inclined to take risks, you ought to be a little careful and watch this around age 25'. Adverse health indications can be handled by assuring the person of basic good health and vitality, but warning that at a certain age more care has to be taken than usual, a little more relaxation at that time would help.

Remember that it is the combined indications you see in the hand which will help you to arrive at the true picture. You are the artist who has to produce a portrait and you can only do this by combining the deductions you gain from the major signs and marks in the hand. Never go on one indication alone.

Always end on an encouraging note, everyone has something to develop and some good fortune coming their way – stress this.

CHAPTER THREE

THE HAND

When we spoke about delineating the hand we advised you to look at the back of the raised hands.

The shape of the hands is informative. Much can be gleaned as to temperament and characteristic behaviour.

There are FIVE BASIC TYPES:

1. *The Square hand.* It really is more or less square and does describe its owner well, as in the modern parlance 'a square'. The palm is as wide as it is long, often the fingers are squarish, but they can be long or short and smooth or knotted. The owner of the square hand is a practical, down to earth individual, a realist.

He is a worker, essentially responsible and reliable, the 'salt of the earth'. His faults are that he is resistant to change, he can be a creature of habit, even dull, but on the whole his virtues of solid worth and achievement outweigh his failings. His are the hands of success and can belong to either sex, but are usually male. The business man or the good housekeeper both have square hands.

If there is a pronounced curve on the outer edge of the palm, these people are creative in a practical, constructive way. In general the square hand has few lines and these are straight.

They are people of integrity with no extremes.

SQUARE   CONIC   SPATULATE

POINTED   MIXED

2. *The Conic hand*. The conic hand has round fingers and a rounded base to the hand. The fingers taper and the thumb often bends outwards. The lines show more variation than on the square hand.

These hands are often seen on the Latin races, also on the Irish.

The owner of the conic hand appreciates art and beauty and they make good hosts or hostesses for the conic hand is basically female

These people pick up knowledge quickly, but tend to be superficial, they are talkative, likeable and can influence others. With knotty fingers the conic hand owner may be of an original inventive mind, and have more staying power than the smooth-fingered folk.

3. *The Pointed hand*. Often called the 'psychic'. This is a beautiful hand of delicacy and grace and it rightly describes its owners as such. The unfortunate part is that these people are relatively useless in the hard world of reality.

They are partly of this world only, the world never understands them nor they the world. They have an interest in the arts and often in psychic matters, but energy is lacking to produce anything creative. If the fingers are knotted, their lives are much luckier for they can become involved in the

field of music, show business or anything to
do with beauty culture.

4. *The Spatulate hand*. This hand is narrower
at the base than at the top of the palm. The
fingers are broad (spade shaped), at the tips.

These are the hands of the individualist,
the inventor and the mechanical genius.
Science and engineering are their field and
they love activity and travel. Their lives are
subject to change and they do not in general
make stable companions. but they are
interesting company.

Women with this type of hand are firm
believers in 'do it yourself', they are always
active and ingenious, versatile and capable.

5. *The Mixed hand*. This is a definite type in
itself and is often seen today for it is the hand
of versatility. The palm combines qualities of
the foregoing types and the fingers are
diversified. These hands combine creativity
with practicality and are often found on the
business side of the creative arts.

There are certain other factors to be
assessed which may be mentioned briefly.

Hand size. This must be judged in relation
to body size, assessment comes with
experience. In general it can be said that the
smaller the hand, the bigger the ideas and
yet the less keen the person is on carrying out
his ideas himself, especially if the hands are

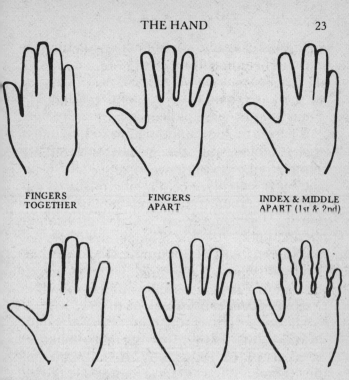

FINGERS
TOGETHER

FINGERS
APART

INDEX & MIDDLE
APART (1st & 2nd)

SUN & LITTLE FINGER
APART (3rd & 4th)

SMOOTH

KNOTTED

also smooth. The owner of the small hand thinks and acts quickly.

Large hands slow down a person's thought and action, a more analytical, thoughtful disposition is present particularly if the finger joints are also knotted. These people like to carry out their own ideas.

The Handshake. This ideally should be firm

and elastic, not *too* firm for this shows you that the person is trying to impress you. Nor should it be too soft and fleshy for this shows a nature that likes luxury, can be sensual and indolent, may want to lean on you.

A hard, dry hand shows overmuch emotional control, the person is probably self-centred, nervy and worrisome.

Hand colour. The colour of the hands tell you about the vitality and activity of the person. Pale hands show lack of vitality, circulation is sluggish. Temperament is cool and there is lack of enterprise. The owner of the hand whose basic tinge is yellow often has a rather jaundiced outlook on life, pessimism and caution colour the outlook.

The owner of the pink hand is in the happy position of being a normal healthy, enterprising individual. With the owner of the red hand you have normal activity 'revved' up too much, there is too much push and go, the red hand shows an aggressive nature and overactivity.

Flexibility. The general rule is that the flexible relaxed hand which bends backwards and forwards easily at the wrist and whose fingers are not stiff and unbendable belongs to the adaptable, easygoing, companionable, progressive person. The stiffer the hands and fingers the less easily accepting is the person, a stiff *hand* often shows a stiff *mind*.

Skin texture. A fine skin shows a finer more sensitive nature than is shown by a coarse skin texture.

Hand spread. While you have the person's hands held up before you with the backs towards you, you have the opportunity to glean much from the way they hold the fingers.

(1) If the fingers are held together, you have a person who is very conventional and rather sensitive.

(2) If the fingers are all apart then you can say here is an unconventional person, who values freedom and is generous and rather bohemian.

(3) If there is a space between the first and second finger then the person thinks for himself.

(4) If there is a space between the third and fourth fingers then you have a person who values freedom of action especially in their private life – too conventional a marriage just will not suit.

(5) If all the fingers fall in towards the palm, you have someone who is very tenacious and wants to hold on to people and possessions. They are reserved and careful moneywise.

(6) A wide gap between thumb and first finger shows a generous, independent, outgoing character.

(7) Knuckled fingers, that is where you can see the joints pronounced, unless this is caused by rheumatism or some other disease of the joints, point to the person who thinks a great deal, these

people reason and do not act on impulse or inspiration as do those whose fingers are smooth.

Finally remember that in the right handed person the left hand is the hand of their private inner life, the hand of the unconscious, the right hand of the outward self, the person they show to the world. You will often find that these are markedly different, namely that their attitudes differ as to whether they are dealing with their families or their employer and the general public. Naturally the reverse will apply if the person is left handed.

CHAPTER FOUR

ALL ABOUT THE FINGERS

Many points of value to be gathered from observation of the fingers are dealt with in the last chapter, for palmistry is above all good observation plus learning the meaning of what you observe about the way the person holds their hands, the shape of the hands, fingers and the markings on the palm.

Probably the thing that you notice first about the fingers is whether they are too long or short in relation to the palm.

This gives you an important piece of information about the person for it indicates broadly whether a person is an intellectual, emotional or material/physical thinker.

You can take it that the fingers are long in relation to the palm when the longest finger is as long as the palm itself. It is considered normal if the longest finger is about seven-eighths the length of the palm.

Short fingers are of course shorter than this is relation to the palm and with experience you will get to know whether they fall under the heading of emotional or material/physical thinking.

Long fingers point to a capacity for abstract thought, detail and exactitude.

Short fingered people are quicker in thought, more impatient of detail, they see things as a whole.

With long slim fingers the intellect is in control, with short strong fingers the emotional/physical nature rules.

Smooth fingers are the fingers of intuition and inspiration, knotty fingers always imply analysis, criticism and a less companionable nature, however their owners gain in stability and a more serious outlook on life.

Thick fingers, like thick hands, show emotional force and energy, and fingers which are thick and fleshy as they emerge from the palm show that their owners like the delights of the table and are luxury lovers in general.

Finger length has also to be considered in the relation of one finger to others on the hand.

The Index Finger

This is also called the Jupiter finger, this is normal in length when it is equal in length to the third or Apollo finger, giving balance and confidence to the nature. If a little shorter it

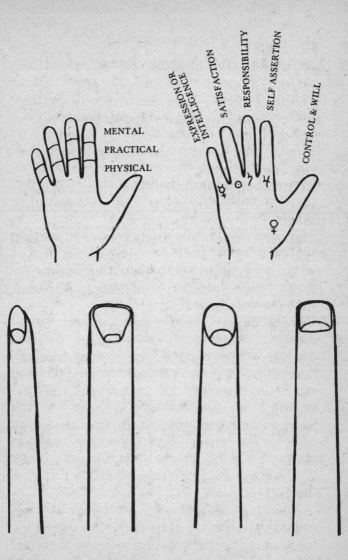

MENTAL
PRACTICAL
PHYSICAL

EXPRESSION OR INTELLIGENCE
SATISFACTION
RESPONSIBILITY
SELF ASSERTION
CONTROL & WILL

POINTED   SPATULATE   CONIC   SQUARE

shows a person of some reserve, who is not inclined to boss others or too keen to take vast responsibility, but will work well in partnership and be quite happy sharing work and glory with others.

An index finger considerably longer than the third finger shows confidence and an outward going personality. This person likes the limelight, has a tendency to dominate others.

A very short index finger shows a deep seated inferiority complex especially if it is also a long tie with the head and life line (of which more later in the chapter on lines), and a low set little finger.

In any case a very short index finger always points to a cautious and retiring nature, while an index finger longer than the ring or Apollo finger gives extravert and leadership qualities.

The index finger which curls in towards the middle finger shows a very retiring and self-effacing nature and even lack of pride and self-respect, for the index finger – being the finger of Jupiter – rules the good things of life and the ability to acquire them.

It is the finger of success, authority, happiness.

The Middle or Saturn Finger

May be called the Balance Wheel of the hand, it stands for responsibility in life and a person's attitude to this. Overlong and heavy in relation to the other fingers, namely dominating the hand, it shows a serious outlook and foreshadows a life of many restrictions and responsibilities, these people do not attain success easily.

Straight and in proportion to the rest of the fingers neither overlong nor overshort, it shows prudence and a reasonable attitude to life and its responsibilities.

The overshort Saturnian finger suggests a lack of inner strength and a certain irresponsibility, these people are often unconventional and some gravitate to the artistic or journalistic fields.

The Ring or Sun Finger

As mentioned earlier, when the Jupiter and Sun fingers are of the same length the character possesses balance and self-confidence. The Sun finger is the finger of creativity, art, success, fame and fulfilment.

A very long Sun finger, nearly equal to the Saturn finger points to the gambler with love, money, life; the person with a long Sun finger cannot live without excitement and stimulus.

A short Sun finger shows that the

Jupiterian ambitions will dominate, the artistic and cultural side of life will be pushed to one side, the person will be always on the wheel of achievement.

A leaning of the Sun finger to the Saturn finger points to emotional immaturity, an unrealistic approach to love.

The Little or Mercury Finger

This is the finger of self-expression, both mental and physical. It rules intellect and both professional and commercial activities.

The Mercury finger is normal in length when it reaches halfway up the nail phalange of the Sun finger. Self expression is adequate, there is speed of thought and action.

If the finger is longer than this you find the person with a lively intelligence and a versatile interesting manner of expression. If the nail phalange is longer than the other two you have the writer and story-teller.

A short Mercury finger is a definite obstacle in life for we all need to be able to communicate adequately; it is specially difficult in marriage.

If you want to know whether a person is a good business man or woman look and see whether the little finger curves slightly inward towards the Sun finger. This is the sign of a shrewd business brain.

In each finger the top section is taken as representing ideals and emotions, the middle section, mentality and powers of coordination, the lower section of the material/ practical and physical.

When doing a reading it is necessary to relate the affairs governed by the individual finger. If for instance you find that the third section of the middle finger is the longest then you know that the person is good at managing money, for the lower section of each finger deals with the practical and material spheres of life.

If the middle section of the Apollo finger is the longest, then in the sphere of art the business side of art and entertainment will attract.

Relate too the shape of the fingers to the meaning of each individual finger for you will sometimes find the Mixed finger type, which is the versatile person, although normally the shape of the fingers should tally with the hand shape. That is to say that a square hand would ideally have square fingers, a pointed hand, pointed fingers, a conic hand, conic fingers, the spatulate hand, spade shaped fingertips.

Square fingers show practicality and realism according to the affairs governed by that finger.

Conic fingers show impulse and imagination, again related to that particular finger.

Pointed fingers show artistic inclinations, intuition and often impracticality, these people are restless and changeable.

Spatulate fingers show energy, enterprise and originality.

A person with square tips on a square hand would be a very 'square' person indeed, a complete realist.

A square hand would be improved by conic fingertips, giving a more imaginative and beauty loving nature.

There is a saying in palmistry circles that 'fingers are best worn straight' and this is very true. Straight fingers show the person to be straightforward, honest and principled. If the fingers are widespread the person is too outspoken, perhaps.

Crooked, the finger shows some deviousness, naturally unless this is due to accident and injury, in the affairs related to that finger.

When you have sized up the fingers for shape, size and section length, relate all these findings to the matters ruled by each finger.

Then look to see whether the fingers when the hand is raised are widespread or held close together.

If widespread, the person is more open, confident and freedom loving.

If close together the opposite holds, the person is reserved, close with money, lacking in confidence, secretive and rather conventional.

If the index and middle fingers cling, the person will achieve success through their work.

If the third and middle fingers cling, the person is insecure emotionally, rather immature and needs a prop.

These people like to work in large organizations. This gives them a feeling of belonging, for instance in either civic, governmental, the armed or nursing services.

If the little finger stands apart from the hand the person needs independence workwise, and even within a close relationship.

The nails can give you some valuable information about the owner of the hand.

The square finger has a broad square nail, the conic finger has an oval nail, the pointed finger an almond shaped nail, the spatulate finger has a nail with a narrow base which broadens towards the tip.

Short nails show the owner has energy, curiosity, intuition, broad nails show good judgement and clarity of thought. Long almond-shaped nails show less energy but the owners are more easy-going.

Pale nails show lack of vitality, coldness and possibly a selfish disposition. Pink nails show good vitality, warmth and a kindly disposition. Too red nails can indicate aggression.

The presence of Moons on the nails is a good indication, showing a strong heart and good circulation.

Mr Johnson of Canada, an experienced palmist of many years standing, told me he had found something interesting relating particularly to the male which goes 'No moons, no stay' and can often be taken as an indication of the perpetual bachelor. With women it is said to indicate a dull marriage.

White spots on the nails indicate a tired and run-down constitution – there is need to let up and take a holiday.

Longitudinal ridges on the nails point to a tendency to contract rheumatism and an over-tense nervous system.

On the whole, sound nails of good colour indicate good health and temper.

CHAPTER FIVE

THE THUMB AND MOUNT OF VENUS

It is said that the Indian palmist can read the character and life story of his client in the thumb.

True or not, it is certain that the development of the human thumb has been closely linked with invention and technological development. Consider that anything which has to be grasped depends upon grip and the use of thumb power for conscious direction and it is the latter combined with will and reasoning power which the thumb stands for in the hand. For this reason it is the key to character and destiny.

Length: the thumb should be reasonably long. That is, it should reach well above the first joint of the index finger when laid close to this finger for measurement. Another guide is that the nail section should be the longest section in the hand, namely, longer than any of the finger sections, for this will give the person power of direction over his life.

It should be firm, well proportioned and moderately flexible.

The angle at which the thumb is normally held in relation to the hand is important. When the hand is spread out, the thumb should stand out from the palm at a reasonable distance, but not too far, a wide angle shows generosity, independence, love of liberty.

Too wide angled a thumb shows a very asocial tendency, selfishness and a desire for

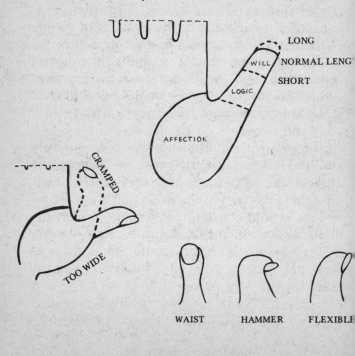

LONG

WILL — NORMAL LENG

SHORT

LOGIC

AFFECTION

CRAMPED

TOO WIDE

WAIST   HAMMER   FLEXIBL

complete freedom of action.

When the thumb is held close to the hand you have someone who is cold, selfish and close with money, also lacks independence.

The rule is, the larger the thumb the stronger the moral force, self-control and intelligence, small thumbs show a weak impressionable nature.

The *set* of the thumb can tell you something important. The higher set the thumb, the less intelligent and the more selfish the person. A low set thumb has a definite bearing on physical skill and coordination.

Thumbs, like fingers, can be flexible or inflexible at the tips and the rules are the same, flexibility shows a sociable, lively, adaptable, easy-going nature. Stiff thumbs, like stiff fingers, show rigidity of mind, caution and reliability. The owners of flexible thumbs and fingers are observant and do well in jobs requiring observation and adaptability, like journalism.

Too supple a thumb shows the person to be too easily influenced by others.

The thumb is traditionally divided into three sections, the top, nail section representing will power, the second section representing reason. The bottom section, which is called the Mount of Venus

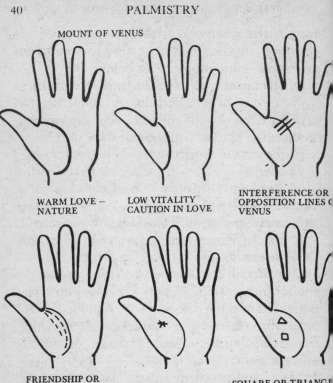

MOUNT OF VENUS

WARM LOVE –
NATURE

LOW VITALITY
CAUTION IN LOVE

INTERFERENCE OR
OPPOSITION LINES O
VENUS

FRIENDSHIP OR
LOVELINES ON
VENUS

STAR ON VENUS

SQUARE OR TRIANGI
ON VENUS

represents the love nature and the person's natural vitality.

When judging the thumb, the ideal is that the first and second sections should be equal, for a long first section and a short second section makes for impulse, while with a short first section and a long second section too much thought can choke action and so produce inertia. Such people are cautious and make good advisers for others.

A strong full top section shows wilfulness and a 'me first' attitude. A thick second section does not make for tact or diplomacy, as does the thin-waisted second section.

Some time you may encounter the 'hammer thumb', a very thick first section and one can only say 'beware' for such people *can* be violent and in any case are extremely stubborn. In a woman's hand this can be a hereditary factor without any adverse psychological trait attached.

The Mount of Venus is the third section of the thumb, that fleshy ball at its base encircled by the life line. It represents our capacity for love, including sexual love, friendship and our appreciation of beauty and the good things of life.

Men and women with a high firm, full Mount of Venus are highly sexed. To them love, marriage, the home and children are important. How the desire nature is controlled will be told you by the strength of the thumb and the headline. Unless there are other negative indications in the hand this is the hand of fertility and vitality.

A high soft mount shows an excitable, changeable nature.

A small flat Mount of Venus shows self-containment and detachment. A low vital force evidently does not allow them to give out much to others. This is not a good augury for a large family.

The shape of the thumb, like the shape of the fingers, also affects the attitude to life. Smooth-jointed thumbs show less thought than knotty ones.

Square-tipped thumbs show a realistic nature, pointed thumbs, especially if smooth too, show impulse and impracticality.

Finally, a high Mount of Venus will give a hollow palm which – according to some palmists – is lucky since it has a holding capacity, to others it indicates over-caution, fear of life and a desire for non-comittal, which in operation can lead to no life at all to speak of. But the hollow hand of the traditional palmists is a thin hand and should not be confused with the hollow hand caused by high mounts.

CHAPTER SIX

THE MOUNTS AND THEIR MEANINGS

Underneath the fingers lie the Mounts – as fleshy elevations – and palmistry traditionally assigns to them, as to the fingers, astrological names in keeping with the fingers whose base they form.

The Mounts, by their development or the

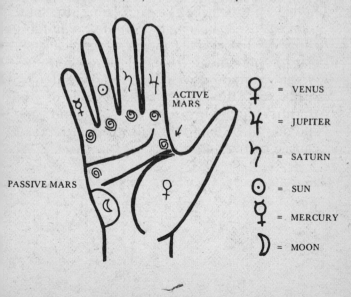

ACTIVE MARS

PASSIVE MARS

♀ = VENUS

♃ = JUPITER

♄ = SATURN

⊙ = SUN

☿ = MERCURY

☽ = MOON

MOUNT OF JUPITER

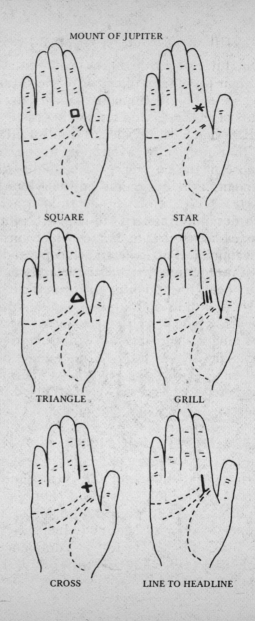

SQUARE

STAR

TRIANGLE

GRILL

CROSS

LINE TO HEADLINE

lack of it, by their firmness or flabbiness and by their placement under or to the side of the fingers, show developed or under-developed traits of character and lines of interest.

If developed, the special quality attached to that particular Mount is strong in the nature, if the development is slight or non-existent, that particular trait or interest is latent.

Lines running to Mounts tell you the special area of interest to which personal development and experience is directed, they are landmarks and save you from scratching your head too much as to the meaning of a particular line or marking on the Mounts, that is, if you have firmly in your head the meaning of the particular Mount, and it is as necessary to know the meaning of the Mounts as it is to understand the area of character and experience symbolized by the fingers.

THE MOUNT OF JUPITER

Jupiter in astrology is called the Greater Fortune and stands for the great benefits of life, for pride, position, honour and opportunity. The person who has a strong Jupiter finger and Mount (which lies below the index finger), is full of confidence and optimism, everything will turn out well, they think. Its presence points to a fine position and a happy marriage. When the Mount drifts towards the Saturn finger and is found more in the space between the Jupiter and Saturn finger, joy and confidence are less, but achievements can be more solid, conservative and worthwhile.

One can have too much of a good thing though and this is shown by an over-developed Jupiter Mount high, soft and broad it shows self-indulgence, a wastrel tendency.

A flat Mount of Jupiter is an indication of a lack of generosity, of consideration, a lazy person who can lack self-respect or ambition.

There are marks and symbols on the hand which all tell us something and some of these are found on the Mounts.

Marks on the Jupiter Mount:

The Square on Jupiter, this marking protects the owner's worldly position and goods.

A Triangle is a symbol of good luck and success.

A Star shows great happiness in married life and a high position.

A Cross shows a romantic love attachment which will in some way advance its owner's position in life.

A Grille shows bossiness and egotism.

MOUNT OF SATURN

SQUARE

TRIANGLE

STAR

GRILL

CROSS

CIRCLE

Since Jupiter has to do with money, position and opportunity, a line running from this mount to the line of Head (see Chapter Seven on lines), shows intense interests in financial advancement.

THE MOUNT OF SATURN

To be happy, this Mount should really be conspicuous by its absence.

This is the Mount which, if developed, lies directly under the Saturn or middle finger. When we spoke of the fingers we noted that the finger of Saturn represented duty, work, business responsibility and stability – so does the Mount.

The Line of Fate or Destiny which we shall be discussing later is directed towards this finger and the stronger the line, Mount, and finger of Saturn, the more restricted by temperament, duty and responsibility the life.

When the area beneath the Saturn finger is flat it shows that the Saturnian traits of pessimism and melancholy are not strong in the nature.

When there is a well-developed Mount, we have the serious, introspective, brooding, reserved type. He has little warmth of personality and so rarely marries and if he does it is usually late in life.

MOUNT OF SUN

STAR

CROSS

TRIANGLE

SQUARE

GRILL

The larger the Mount of Saturn the more the morbid, introspective melancholy side of the nature is developed.

When the line of Heart begins on this Mount we have a person to whom the physical side of love is important as they find it difficult to communicate lovingly to others except through the physical medium. They are short on the niceties of life and can be termed selfish.

Marks and symbols on the Mount of Saturn:

A *Square* gives job protection and protects against financial worries.

A *Triangle* shows an interest in the scientific and the occult, a mind suited to research.

A *Star* hints at a dramatic fate.

A *Grille* increases the depressive tendencies of a high Mount.

A *Cross* as a distinct mark can point to a sudden end.

A *Circle* shows isolation.

THE MOUNT OF THE SUN

Like the Sun finger under which it lies, this Mount has much to do with the Arts, the finer things of life, with the field of public entertainment, with sociability and prestige.

Well-developed it indicates a pleasant,

sunny disposition, a love of beauty and artistic abilities. With a good line of Sun it brings success in the Arts; theatre, painting, writing, dancing and music.

When this Mount drifts towards the Saturn finger you have a more serious approach allied to the creative faculty – possibly the writer or composer rather than the actor.

With a drift towards the little finger you have someone who is able for or engaged in the business side of the artistic field, a production manager, director, publisher perhaps.

An over-developed Mount gives talent, but affectation, extravagance, emotional instability and love of attention. They dream too much and achieve too little.

A flat Mount of the Sun points to someone who has little interest in aesthetic values, lacks imagination, but probably makes up for it in practicality.

Marks and symbols on the Mount of the Sun:

A *Star* on the Mount is a happy sign of good augur for it signals wealth, prestige, success probably in the artistic field. Success comes through talent and the help of influential people.

A *Cross* is not so happy for it symbolizes

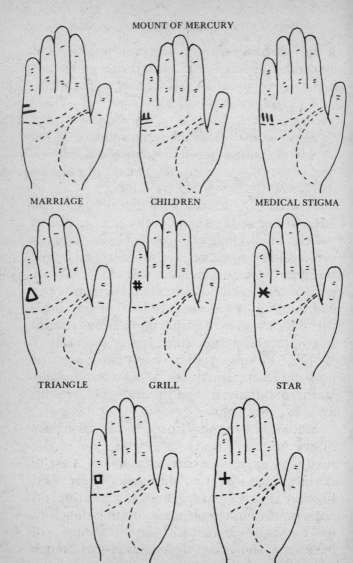

MOUNT OF MERCURY

MARRIAGE   CHILDREN   MEDICAL STIGMA

TRIANGLE   GRILL   STAR

SQUARE   CROSS

dashing of one's hopes, however, if the line of Sun continues beyond this point all is not lost.

A *Triangle* is a lucky omen of stable success.

The Square protects the reputation.

A *Grill* shows one who pushes too hard.

THE MOUNT OF MERCURY

This is the Mount which lies beneath the Mercury or little finger.

Mercury in mythology was the Messenger of the Gods, so basically the Mercury finger and the Mercury Mount inform us how a person will communicate. Although the Mercury finger is the smallest finger, both the Mount and the finger symbolize many things largely to do with expression, such as writing, talking, selling, everyday practical and commercial affairs. It also symbolizes science, business, health and the healing arts.

Since the Mercury finger lies in that part of the hand which is an expression of the instinctive self (see illustration No. 1), the development of the Mercury Mount and finger can also have a very big bearing on happiness in marriage and close relationship.

The well-developed firm Mount of Mercury shows a lively, practical active person, someone who would do well in industry or business, especially anything to do with travel and communications.

With a good, but slightly curved inward Mercury finger we have the shrewd business brain, someone who makes money. To the strongly Mercurian type, variety is not only the spice of life, but a necessity.

Undeveloped, we have the impractical, muddled person, a person who is 'heavy on the hand'. Over-developed we have the 'con' man, who likes an easy life and easy money, this is sure to be true if the Mercury finger is also crooked.

When the Mount drifts towards the Sun finger, we have someone who has a practical interest in the arts, a possible choice of career would be in the antique field.

When the Head line points towards this Mount we have the collector of things and knowledge.

There are various signs and symbols on the Mercury Mount which are of importance in hand analysis. Here we find the lines of marriage and children, also the medical stigmata consisting of a few straight short lines. With a good Mercury finger and the rest of the fingers also good and thick, we have the indications of one who would make a doctor, nurse or social worker. Its presence also shows one who is sympathetic and will help others in need.

Minor Marks on the Mount:

A Triangle shows success in business.

A Grille points to cunning or dishonesty.

A Star points to success in examinations, as a scientist or inventor.

MOUNT OF MOON

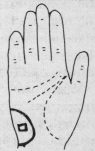

HEADLINE DROPS   STAR   SQUARE
TO THE MOON

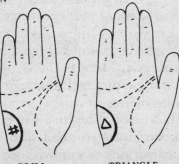

GRILL   TRIANGLE

A Cross can mean double dealing and is a warning against this from others.

A Square shows protection against mental strain.

From the Mercury Mount starts the line of Health and success in business.

THE MOUNT OF THE MOON

The Mount of the Moon lies on the far side of the hand and opposite the thumb.

You can see whether this Mount is developed or not by the fact that the outer edge of the palm will curve if it is and this is always called the creative curve, for the Mount of the Moon is the area of imagination and creativity.

A firm developed Mount of the Moon denotes sensitivity and a fertile, creative imagination. The line of the Sun usually begins in this area and shows the imagination leading to success in the creative field.

Lines of travel and of restlessness are also marked on the Mount of the Moon, the person voyages in imagination or in fact to faraway places.

Where you find a high soft overdeveloped Mount of the Moon you will find the moody, touchy, changeable person, who live in their dreams and whose emotional relationships are always up and down due to their own inconstancy.

A flat Mount (a hand where the edge is straight up and down) indicates that there is less imagination, sympathy and warmth. These people tend to get set in their ways mentally and physically early in life and stay so.

When the Mount of Luna drops into the wrist the person has an awareness of rhythm in life and nature.

Sometimes the Head line dips towards the Mount of the Moon, here we have creativity and imagination for use as in the writer or artist.

The Head line should not dip too far though or there will be too much dreaming and disconnection with reality, which can lead to mental instability.

Minor Marks on the Mount:

A *Star* on the Mount shows brilliant imagination.

A *Square* gives protection in travel.

A *Grille* shows worries and imaginary fears.

A *Triangle* on the hands of a creative person shows success.

THE MOUNTS OF MARS

There are two Mars Mounts and as Mars is

ACTIVE MARS

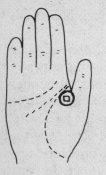

SQUARE

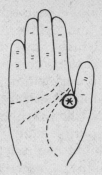

STAR

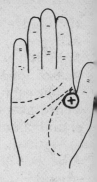

CROSS

PASSIVE MARS

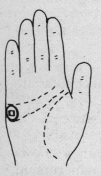

SQUARE

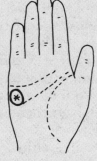

STAR

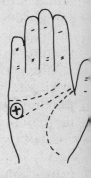

CROSS

the God of war, we have one which shows active courage and aggression, the will to fight, the other which shows the more passive side of Mars, endurance.

The active lower Mount of Mars lies beneath the Mount of Jupiter, above the thumb and below the Life line.

With this Mount strongly developed, we have the person with physical courage and plenty of fight, overdeveloped the quarrelsome bully, flat we have the coward.

The other Mount lies above the Mount of the Moon, on the outside of the palm, between the Head and Heart lines.

This Mount developed shows self-control and overdeveloped shows bad temper and a sarcastic bent.

An undeveloped Upper Mount again shows timidity.

The active or lower Mount of Mars has a great deal to do with vitality, its moderate development adding to the vital force, therefore it is excellent for success in competitive sport.

A square on either mount shows protection from enemies, a star achievement from one's own strength of will. A cross shows secret or open enemies.

CHAPTER SEVEN

THE MAJOR LINES – YOUR PERSONAL MAP

THE LIFE LINE

The Life line will be found on all hands. It begins at the edge of the palm between the thumb and index finger and encircles the Venus Mount, the fleshy pad at the base of the thumb.

THE MAJOR LINES

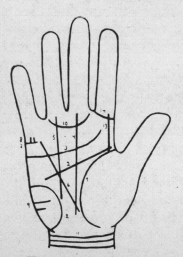

KEY:

1 = LIFE LINE
2 = HEAD LINE
3 = HEART LINE
4 = FATE LINE
5 = SUN LINE
6 = HEALTH LINE
7 = MARRIAGE LINE
8 = CHILDREN
9 = TRAVEL LINES
10 = SENSITIVITY LINE
11 = GOOD FORTUNE
12 = INTUITION LINE
13 = MONEY
14 = SPIRITUALITY

Its beginning, the length and depth of its marking, whether it is broken, crossed or chained, will tell you about the vitality and possibility longevity, although depth and strength of the line taken with other factors showing vitality in the hand, such as the Venus and Mars Mounts may often mean more than a very long line completely encircling the Venus Mount.

Especially strengthening is a line which follows it closely, something for quite a long way, this is known as a Mars line and given additional strength and resistance.

Likewise if the Life line forks at the base of this, again this is a sign of strong resistance to disease.

However, you can take it that if you see a long, clear Life line, free from chains, breaks and islands, then the owner has plenty of vitality and a strong constitution and is likely to make old bones.

The sweep of the Life line is important, showing far more force and drive than when the Life line comes down straight and so narrows the space of the Venus Mount.

The beginning of the Life line gives valuable information about character and life approach. The normal beginning to the Life line is under the Mount of Jupiter, but if it begins *on* that Mount then the person is

MARKINGS ON THE LIFE LINE

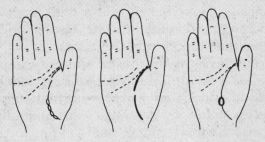

CHOPPED AND
CHAINED

BREAK

ISLAND

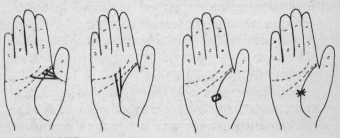

LINES CROSSING
LINES

UPWARD

SQUARE

STAR

extremely ambitious and – unless the thumb and headline are weak – will reach his life goals.

Since markings on the Life line show events and forces which effect the life for good or ill it is wise to know when to expect them, then it is possible to look forward to the good happenings and to ease the brunt of the more difficult.

The hand seems to go along with the biblical 'four score years and ten' and seventy years on the Life line is about an inch above the thick base of the palm.

The easiest way to find time on the Life line is to divide it up into ten-year sections, remembering that the line starts under the Jupiter Mount so that your first three divisions will represent youth – up to thirty years of age.

The next three divisions will carry you through the middle years and the last ten years will represent age, if the line continues past your seventy mark then longevity is indicated.

Markings on the Life Line

The chained or much chopped up Life is not a good health indication. It can mean general poor health, accidents, allergies or spinal trouble.

A real break in the Life line shows an accident or serious ill-health.

An island indicates the time to take things more easily, there will be less vital force.

Lines crossing the Life line show emotional or family worries and anxieties. These are known as lines of experience.

A square as usual gives protection when it is needed. Upward moving lines are always

TYPE OF LIFE LINE

 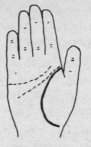 

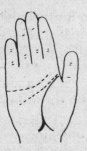

1. YOUTH
2. MIDDLE LIFE
3. LATE LIFE

LONG LIFELINE

LONG BUT
NOT CLEAR

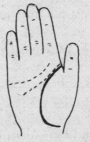

FORKED

STRONG VITALITY

DOUBLE

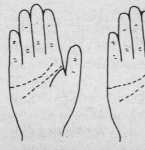 

SHORT BUT
UNCLEAR

SHORT BUT
CLEAR

good, they show progress and enterprise, the ability to recuperate from illness. A star always indicates a life crisis, whether of health or progress.

A study of the Life line gives much information about the character and life of the person, but should never be considered without reference to the rest of the lines and the hand type in general.

THE HEAD LINE

The Head line is one of the main indications of the type of intelligence the person possesses. In comparison with the Heart line it shows whether the head or heart rules.

The Head line begins like the Life line on the side of the hand between the thumb and index finger.

Its manner of beginning is important:

1. Joined to the Life line lightly shows thoughtfulness and prudence. This is not a person of extremes.

2. Joined to the Life line for about half-an-inch. Where you find this you discover the ultra cautious, rather fearful person who follows the teachings of his elders and the majority way of thinking. He is usually slow to make changes and lacking in confidence.

3. Where you find the Head line separated narrowly from the Life line, you have a more

enterprising, confident, original way of looking at life – these people can and do take risks, they are impulsive.

4. Where the Life line and the Head line are widely separated in both hands it suggests recklessness, extreme impulse and restlessness, these people find it hard to stick at anything for long.

Where the Head line starts just inside the Life line on the Mount of Mars, you have a sensitive excitable and touchy character.

You may find that a person has one indication on one hand and another on the other. In which case there will always be conflict, one side of the nature pulling against the other and the person will exhibit traits of independence at one time and extreme lack of confidence in other situations.

When assessing the Head line, it is wise to remember that all straight lines show control so a short straight line will show a basically practical shrewd mind – many business men have these.

A long straight Head line will show preoccupation with detail and a capacity to organize and control the mind to given ends, in fact the ability to concentrate.

It is true to say that the average man has a curved Heart line and a straight Head line,

HEAD LINE

1. YOUTH
2. MIDDLE LIFE
3. LATE LIFE

JOINING
LIFELINE

WIDE SEPARATION
FROM LIFELINE

LONG AND
STRAIGHT

CURVING DOWN

SHORT

BEGINNING IN
UPPER MARS

SMALL
SEPARATION

CHAINED

BREAK

LINE FROM
HEAD TO HEART

LIGHT,
UNCLEAR

LINES
CROSSING

while the reverse holds true for the average woman.

The curving down of the Head line shows imagination and intuition and we all know about 'women's intuition', which also bears out the fact that in general women have sloping headlines.

On the square practical hand you will usually find the straight Head line showing an excellent logical, realistic mind, and when you find a sloping one you can say that the person will use his or her intuitive, creative gifts in a practical and constructive manner.

The Conic hand usually has a sloping Head line so if you find that there is a straight Head line, then the usual flair for self-expression, the creative and inventive turn of mind shown by the Conic hand will be much muted and turned to more mundane, practical or technical matters.

Where you find a wide fork at the end of the sloping Head line, you will find a person who is too versatile and who lacks concentration and single-mindedness.

The same applies if you have the end of the line split into several branches, the person tends to be muddled and confused.

Events can be timed on the Head line as on the Life line, but it is easiest in this case to divide the line up into three sections for youth, adulthood and later life beginning with the start of the line on the palm between the thumb and index finger.

Markings on the Head Line

A light and wavery line shows lack of direction, difficulty in concentrating.

A chained Head line shows worry, anxiety, tension, at the time shown by the chains or islands.

A break in the Head line can show a breakdown, but if enclosed by a square or if the line overlaps, recovery. Little lines crossing show worries and maybe headaches. A line reaching up from the Head line to the Heart line shows the likelihood of an unhappy experience in love, hence from then on a much more hardheaded approach to life.

Many successful people have this line, which marked a turning point in their lives and the beginning of their outward success.

THE HEART LINE

The Heart line indicates the emotional attitudes in the person, warmhearted and giving or cold and introverted.

For most of us this is a very interesting line, showing as it does how we are in love, and what we look for in others to complement ourselves.

There are two horizontal lines in the hand, the lower is the Head line, the upper is the Heart line.

It starts at the opposite edge of the palm to the thumb, under the little finger and runs towards the thumb side of the palm.

In a few hands you will find this line missing, there is only one horizontal line and in this case it is the Head line, namely the Head line and the Heart line are fused.

This shows that the head will rule the heart and that the person has terrific powers of concentration on any given goal. He will achieve whatever he sets out to do, but may lose out on his emotional life in the process.

We noted earlier that the average male hand has a curved Heart line, showing more impulse and less control than a straight one.

The average female hand shows by its straightness a more controlled attitude to love, a slower reaction emotionally.

When the Heart line runs from the edge of the palm right across the hand onto the Jupiter Mount, we find the person who is possessive in love.

When the Heart line curves upwards and finishes between the index and second finger, we have a reasonable, loving attitude,

someone who should make a success of love
and marriage.

When the Heart line stops under the
second, Saturn finger, we have a person who
finds it difficult to express any sort of finesse
or subtlety in love. If this is present in both
hands then the person is naturally selfish and
physical in love. If however, the left hand
shows a curved, much longer Heart line, we
can be sure that childhood experiences were
repressive.

When the Heart line crosses over to the
Jupiter Mount and then dives down to touch
the Head line it indicates great
disappointment in love, but chiefly because
these people seem to lack perception in
knowing whom to love. Their affections are
often misplaced and seldom returned.

However, it should be noted that a long
line of Heart always shows an outward-going
nature, a short line much reserve and
introversion.

A thin line of Heart without branches
shows the person who does not go out to
others.

The chained line shows much
changeability of the affections.

Little branches rising from the Heart line
show affections, little branches dropping
show disappointments.

MARKINGS ON HEART LINE

GIRDLE OF VENUS

CROSSES

COMPLETELY BROKEN

EXPRESSIVE HEART LINE

NARROW SPACE BETWEEN HEART & HEAD

HEART LINE

BRANCHED & CHOPPED

FINISHING BETWEEN 1st & 2nd FINGER

STOPPING UNDER 2nd FINGER

TOUCHING HEADLINE

1. YOUTH
2. MIDDLE LIFE
3. LATE LIFE

CURVED HEART STRAIGHT HEAD

STRAIGHT HEART & CURVED HEAD

LONG & STRAIGHT

THIN LINE

CHAINED

Timing may be done on the Heart line as on the Head line by dividing the line into three sections and taking the beginning as the end of the line wherever it starts and finishing on the edge of the palm under the little finger.

Markings on the Heart Line

Some hands have what is called a Girdle of Venus, which is a semi-circular line, broken or unbroken, running above the Heart line and below the fingers. This is an indication of great sensitivity and is really an addition to the Heart line. This Girdle is often present when there is only a single horizontal line in the hand and this shows a much warmer nature and the capacity to feel affection.

Crosses and breaks on the Heart line show emotional sorrows, sometimes the loss of a lover or the end of an affair. A completely broken Heart line shows a very demanding nature.

While the Heart line shows your approach to other people, and your way of expressing affection, it also shows something more, your appreciation of the arts and your creative capacity, for instance an artist may have quite a short Head line, but an expressive, well marked, branched Heart line.

Do you relate everything in life to yourself? This is shown by the space between the two horizontal lines. Narrow space, self-centred and narrow in outlook, wide space, breadth of mind and vision.

These three lines, life, head and heart, are the major lines of the hand, but there are three other lines which are often found and can be easily located once you have found the three major ones.

THE FATE LINE

The Fate line generally starts at the base of the hand, near the wrist and proceeds up the palm to the base of the second finger.

When the Fate line exists at all it indicates that the person has a direction and purpose in life, is in control of his own destiny and is responsible.

The absence of this line tells of lack of direction or purpose, an inability to fit in with the demands of society and therefore an irresponsible, changeable life; the person is like a twig blown about by every current. It is very important to help a young person who has no Fate line to find a true interest and direction otherwise he will waste his time and talents in fruitless activities. He will be a real rolling stone.

FATE LINE

START INSIDE LIFELINE

JOINED TO LIFE LINE AT BEGINNING

STARTING ON MOON

HEAVY FATE LINE = SECURITY

1. YOUTH
2. MIDDLE
3. LATE

LINE JOINING LIFELINE LATER

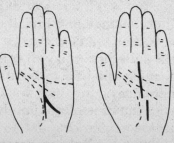

MARRIAGE/PARTNERSHIP, JOINING FATELINE

CHANGE OF JOB OR LIFE

The Fate line does not always begin at the wrist; it can have other beginnings and can be long or short.

1. Beginning inside the Life line – indicates help from parents to get ahead in life.

2. Joined to Life line at the beginning – great family attachment and maybe sacrifice for the parents.

3. Beginning on the Mount of the Moon, opposite the base of the thumb, we have the person whose career is much subject to public approval, can be the entertainer or the politician, someone who both gains and needs approval.

The person in whose hand the Fate line runs up deep and heavy from wrist to the Mount of Saturn is a very independent type. He makes his own decisions and they are always responsible ones, he does not like change, he is an exponent of all that is most responsible in human nature, he loves and craves security.

If this line cuts the hand in half, so heavy is it, then the person tends to get in a rut.

From the Fate line you can read your life and by dividing the line into three you can time your changes.

Take from the base of the hand to the first horizontal line as marking one to thirty, the youthful years, take from the lower horizontal line to the higher as marking the middle period up to about forty-five, take from the upper horizontal line to the base of the fingers as indicating the years from forty-five. Dividing these into sections of ten again will help you time your changes of destiny pattern.

More About the Fate Line

The Fate line running from the base of the wrist up to the Mount of Saturn below the middle finger, shows a person who will always opt for security. In a man this often shows a long career with the same firm, he will work hard, raise a family and retire to enjoy a well merited pension.

Similar markings on a woman's hand may indicate the same, but are more likely to indicate a comfortable secure marriage.

Where the Fate line is joined to the Life line at the start then there is a strong family attachment, or this can mean in these days, an attachment to a community way of living. In any case the young person does not want to leave the group, he wants to belong. When the Life line leaves the Fate line, he finally gains independence.

The Fate line, which starts on the Mount of the Moon opposite the base of the thumb, will be found on the hands of those who depend for their livelihood on the impression they are able to make on the minds and emotions of the masses, that is they work in a personal way with the public.

When the line starts clear at the wrist, then joins the Life line later on, it shows a sacrifice of personal wishes and career for parents or relatives, when the line clears from the Life line the person is able to pursue his own life again.

Marriage or partnership is shown by a line which joins the line of destiny from the Mount of the Moon side of the hand.

Changes in job or career can be seen by a break in the Destiny line and if the lines overlap this will be a successful change.

A branch from the Fate line running to the ring or Apollo fingers shows success in the artistic field.

Markings on the Fate Line

Lines crossing the Fate line show obstacles to be overcome.

Islands or breaks in the Fate line show trouble and uncertainty.

Squares on the Fate line as elsewhere show protection from the worst that Fate can do for you.

If the Fate line doubles, then you have a time of good fortune; this can mean marriage or money or both. In any case you will not be alone.

THE LINE OF SUN OR APOLLO
This is often called the line of success and the least that it can mean in a hand is optimism and satisfaction with one's lot in life.

Public renown can be seen by the line of

SUN LINE

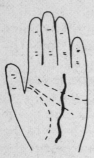

PUBLIC RENOWN   LATE START TO SUN LINE

1. YOUTH
2. MIDDLE
3. LATE

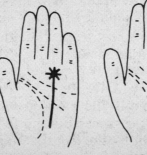

STAR   SQUARE

Sun which starts early in the base of the palm and runs up to the Ring finger. This is the mark of the successful artist or entertainer.

It refers to any accomplishment in the arts or in political life.

This line may be lacking in those who attain fame, but in some way their success will be bitter and they will lack what they feel they deserve.

There are many hands where the line does not start until above the line of heart, this indicates that they find greater happiness and self-expression later in life.

Events can be timed on this line, as on the line of Fate, by division into three sections as before.

Markings on the Sun Line

A long strong Sun line ending in a Star or Triangle destines its owner to fame and fortune. There will be tremendous public recognition of talent.

A Square protects from any adversity or check to the public career.

THE HEALTH LINE

Health is probably the most essential factor in the living of a successful and full life and this is borne out by the fact that in palmistry as in astrology, the areas of health and work

– hence material reward – are linked.

The line of Health starts below the little finger and runs across the palm towards the base of the thumb.

Sometimes it joins the Life line and if it is stronger than the Life line at this point it will be a critical time for the person healthwise.

HEALTH LINE

1. YOUTH
2. MIDDLE
3. LATE

CHOPPED UP

CHAINED

TOUCHING
LIFE LINE

SQUARE

Points to note regarding the health line:

1. This is the line whose absence should bring us joy for it indicates that the person has sound health.

2. Unbroken and strong it indicates good earning capacity, health and excellent business sense.

3. A chopped-up Health line shows indifferent health and possibly – since it has been called the Liver line – digestive problems.

4. Chained or islanded, there will be periods of ill health at the time these occur on the line, maybe hospitalization.

5. A Square shows protection either where business or health is concerned.

In timing events on the Health line remember that the line starts under the little finger so the early years of youth will be represented by the period before the line touches the first horizontal line. The middle years will be represented by the space between the two horizontal lines and the latter years of life by the rest of the line.

CHAPTER EIGHT

WILL YOU BE SUCCESSFUL IN LOVE?

The answer to this is 'yes' if –

1. You have a well developed Mount of Venus, the fleshy pad at the base of the thumb, particularly if the Mount has rising lines on it for this shows warmth and an outgoing temperament, the capacity to give and receive love.

2. You have a long curved well marked Heart line, remember the too-long Heart line, reaching almost to the other side of the palm, is not conducive to happiness in love for it shows a jealous and possessive nature.

3. You have a small Girdle of Venus, the line we mentioned as being the semi-circular marking above the Heart line, for this when small shows emotional sensitivity, the long and broken girdle shows too much tension in love and difficulty in releasing the pent-up feelings.

4. You have a well developed long little finger, it should reach up to or past the line marking the first section of the Sun or Ring

SUCCESS IN LOVE

LOVE LINE

MARRIAGE LINE BEGINNING WITH FORK

ENDING WITH FORK

ENDING IN BARRIER

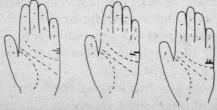

RELATIONSHIP LINES

BREAK BUT CONCILIATION

MARRIAGE & CHILDREN

finger. For the ideal sex partner must not only know how to make love – he must know how to communicate. The possession of a strong little finger indicates that the sex drive is robust, the vitality good.

The indications given above will also hold for finding a suitable mate, which brings us to our next section.

MARRIAGE AND CHILDREN

In a hand which shows some of the markings as given for success in love, marriage or deep affections are shown by a little line (or lines) that start on the side of the hand just below the little finger. These can be long, showing a long marriage, or very short.

Little light lines can be taken as romances, short affairs where the affections are captured, but not held.

Deep lines indicate serious attachments, usually marriage. Where there are two or more lines, the lower they are the earlier they occur in life. The midpoint, between the base of the little finger and the headline is about thirty-seven years of age. One very close to the base of the little finger would indicate marriage very late in life.

Children are marked as little lines which run down into the marriage line.

Often these lines will be found in the

hands of those who have not married or have not had children, but it will always be found that these people love children and have much to do with other people's children.

Assessing Your Marriage Prospects

A long and happy marriage is shown by a long clear, well-cut line.

A number of little lines shows many romances, but little likelihood of marriage.

A marriage line beginning with a fork (shown on the side of the palm) shows a long courtship before marriage takes place.

A fork marked at the end of the marriage line shows that the partners go their own way, they are *separated* in interest if not in fact.

A vertical line crossing the marriage line at the *end* shows the end of the marriage either through divorce or death.

A small line running very close to the marriage line either below or above it shows either an affair just before marriage or one during the duration of the marriage.

A break in a marriage line which later continues shows a break in the marriage, a period of separation, but that the two people will come together again.

If the hand you are reading has none of the markings as given for success in love, then even if there are attachment lines under the little finger, you should be very wary in forecasting marriage for some people are solitary by nature, the confirmed bachelor or bachelor girl often prefers freedom and independence to the marriage tie. In order to know this you have to be able to assess the general warmth and 'outgoingness' of the hand in conjunction with the presence of the marriage lines.

WILL YOU BE LUCKY?

Yes, there is such a thing as luck and this is shown in the hand, where you will find it if you look.

First of all you are generally lucky if you have many Squares marked in your hand for these always indicate providential protection and a sort of charmed life.

There is a marking in the hand called the Angle of Luck and this is formed by the space between the end of the Head line and the end of the Life line. The wider the space between them, the luckier you are. Sometimes you see a narrow space on the person's left hand and a much wider one on the right hand and you can conclude that the person has greatly increased their luck by their own efforts.

Another lucky sign to have is called the Lucky Triangle and is formed by the lines of

Life, Head and Health, since it is similar to the Angle of Luck, again the wider the extent of the triangle, the greater the luck.

If you look carefully at the palm of the hand you will sometimes be able to discern what is called the Lucky M formation. This is shaped by the line of Fate crossing the lines of head and heart and so forming the capital letter M. This has been traditionally taken as

LUCK LINES

ANGLE OF LUCK

LUCKY
TRIANGLE

LUCKY M
FORMATION

LUCK LINES
FROM VENUS

a sign of money/marriage and good fortune in love.

Signs of money luck are shown in the hand by certain lines rising from the Mount of Venus.

A line running upwards from the Mount of Venus to the Mount of Jupiter under the first finger is a good omen. It is a forecast of advancement, promotion, authority and financial success. Lucky portents are heightened when the line ends in a Star.

A line running from the mount of Venus to the base of the second or Saturn finger shows money increase as a result of the person's own efforts and family backing.

A line running from the Mount of Venus to the base of the little finger shows money from commercial or scientific pursuits.

Whoever wins the pools should have a line running from the Mount of Venus to below the third or Sun finger for this line shows windfalls.

TRAVEL LINES

So-called travel lines really show the person's desire to travel and their restlessness, which, other things being equal, i.e., if the opportunity and money is there and there are not too many responsibilities, the person will do.

Travel lines, or lines of restlessness are shown on the Mount of the Moon, on the edge of the palm opposite the Mount of Venus, Many lines, many trips, deep lines, important journeys.

When the Life line at its base forks and one fork points towards the Mount of the Moon, then it is likely that the person will make their home in a country other than the land of their birth.

LINES AND MARKS ON THE PALM

Some hands are clear of all but the major lines, others are criss-crossed with lines and little markings which have a significance in themselves.

In general one cay say that a person with a relatively clear palm is much less nervous and sensitive than the person with many small lines and markings.

Life is an easier matter for the clear-palmed person, since he does not react strongly and is more self-contained and self-centred.

Minor markings on the hand apply to the area in which they are found and affect that area of life for good or ill.

The Minor marks are stars, squares, crosses, islands, triangles, chains, breaks, tassels, forks.

The fortunate signs are squares and stars

indicating protection and good luck, as also does the triangle.

The adverse signs are: chains, islands and circles indicating as they do upsets, restrictions, and difficulties.

A break in the line usually shows a change of direction. A break in the Life, Heart or Head lines is adverse for health.

Tassels at the end of a line show the dispersion of force and are sometimes shown at the end of the Head line. A cross shows adversity or unhappiness, and the fork is similar to the tassel in meaning.

Spiritual Development

These marks should be looked for in the hand for they can have an important bearing on the life and so enable you to slant your reading correctly.

These are the Mystic Cross and Bow of Intuition.

The Mystic Cross lies in the centre of the quadrangle between the lines of Head and Heart.

When present it always shows one whose life consciously or unconsciously will be much influenced by the occult. The person himself may be involved in occult and spiritual work or it may be someone closely related to him.

SPIRITUAL DEVELOPMENT & POTENTIALITIES

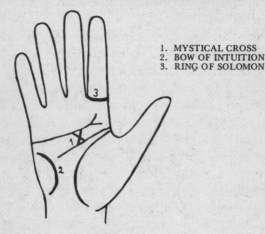

1. MYSTICAL CROSS
2. BOW OF INTUITION
3. RING OF SOLOMON

Another sign which is often present with the Mystic Cross is the Ring of Solomon. This is a line that encircles the base of the index finger and runs from between the index and middle fingers to the outer edge of the palm. Traditionally it is a sign of wisdom and adepthood.

The Bow of Intuition

This is a semi-circular mark and lies in the area of the Mount of the Moon It shows exceptional intuitive and psychic ability and is practically always found on the hands of mediums, psychics and those in whom the E.S.P. faculty is present and developed.

The presence of these signs on the palm

indicates that progress and development along higher lines is possible to the persons, but whether they will always use their gifts in a positive way is entirely up to them.

INDEX